A Magic Mouse Guide

E-mail

by
Chris Ward-Johnson
and the Magic Mouse

Illustrations & layout by
Laughing Gravy Design

CHERRYTREE BOOKS

Editor's note

Computers and e-mail software vary considerably. In this book we present information that is generally true of all PCs and e-mail systems and show a variety of particular screens. Do not worry if your screen is not the same as the one that appears in the book.

Acknowledgments

The publishers would like to thank the following for permission to use their photographs and copyright material:
Eudora; Netscape UK Ltd.

A CHERRYTREE BOOK

Designed and produced by A S Publishing.

Illustrations and layout by Gary Dillon & Phil Jolly
at Laughing Gravy Design Limited.

First published 1999 by Cherrytree Press Ltd
327 High Street
Slough
Berkshire SL1 1TX

In memory of Jonathan Inglis

Copyright this edition © Evans Brothers Ltd 2001

British Library Cataloguing in Publication Data
Ward-Johnson, Chris
E-mail - (Magic Mouse Guides)
Electronic mail systems Juvenile Literature
I. Title
384.3'4

ISBN 1-842-34055-7
Printed and bound in Belgium by
Proost International Book Production.

All rights reserved. No part of this publication may be reproduced, stored in a retrieval system, or transmitted in any form or by any means, without the prior permission in writing of the publisher, nor be otherwise circulated in any form of binding or cover other than that in which it is published and without a similar condition including this condition being imposed on the subsequent purchaser.

Contents

What is e-mail?	4
On the internet	6
E-mail addresses	8
The right address	10
Make it snappy!	12
Say it with a smile	14
Sending your e-mail	16
Looking for a message	18
Receiving a message	20
Attachments	22
Sending a reply	24
Surprise, Surprise!	26
More about e-mail	28
Index	32

Mouse tips

Don't worry if your screen does not always look exactly like the ones in the book.

Mouse tips

If there are words you don't understand, look on pages 28-31.

What is e-mail?

Ben wants to ask Hari to come and play on Tuesday.

If he sends a letter now, it will not get to Hari's house until Wednesday.

Ben asks if he can phone Hari.

Hari is not there. The phone rings and rings. There is no answering machine.

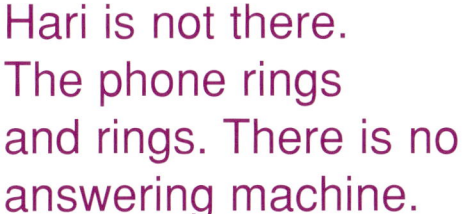

"Why don't you send an e-mail?" says the Magic Mouse.

Sending an e-mail is like sending a letter by telephone.

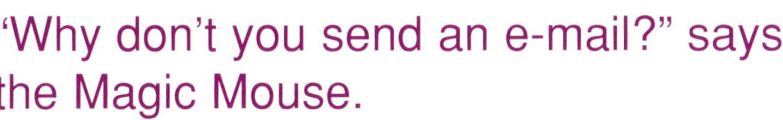

The 'e' in e-mail stands for electronic.

On the internet

"You can use my computer," says Ben's sister Liza.

To send an e-mail, you need a computer, a modem and an e-mail software program.

A modem links your computer to the internet. The internet is like a system of roads in a town. You can go from one address to another on the internet.

The internet is bigger than a town. It links addresses all over the world.

E-mail addresses

Everyone on the internet has an e-mail address. An e-mail address looks like this:

`magic-mouse@evansbrothers.co.uk`

Your address starts with your name, followed by @. The @ sign means 'at'.

The next part of the address is the name of the company that links your computer to the internet.

> An address that contains 'ac' means it is a school or college.

Companies that link people to the internet are called internet service providers, or ISPs.

The letters 'co' stand for company. Guess what 'uk' stands for?

Ben's sister finds Hari's e-mail address.

Never give your e-mail address to anyone you don't know. Never give your real address to anyone either.

The right address

Ben opens the e-mail program on Liza's computer. The screen looks like this:

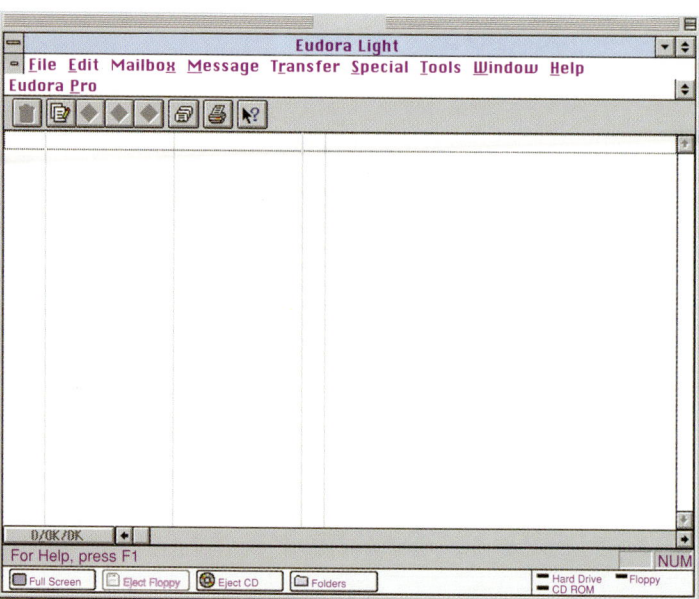

Ben clicks on Message and chooses New Message from the menu.

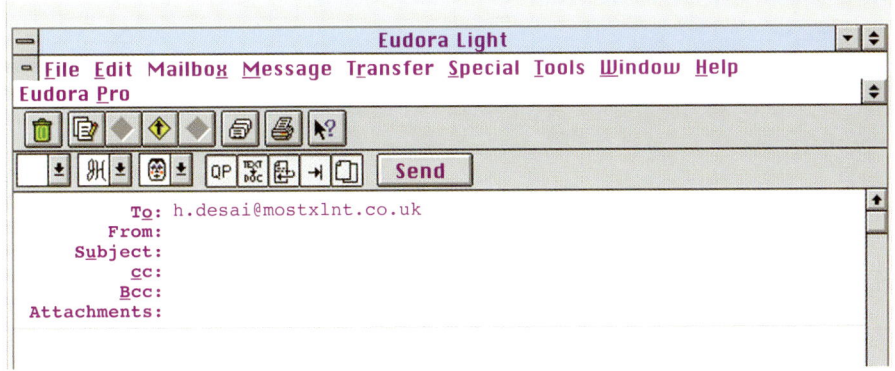

At the top of the window he types in Hari's address and checks it. He makes sure that he has got every letter, word and symbol just right. He remembers to use small letters and not to leave any spaces.

If one dot is out of place in the address, your e-mail will bounce. It will come straight back to your mailbox.

Copy the address exactly. Don't leave gaps.

Make it snappy!

Now Ben writes a subject: Come and play. Underneath he types his message.

```
Dear Hari,
It is my sister's birthday tomorrow. She is going out with all her friends in the afternoon. If you come and play, we will have the house to ourselves. Liza says we can play on her computer. Please reply, so that I can tell Mum.

See you
Ben.
```

SHOUT

Ben makes his message as short as possible. Short messages go quicker. He uses mostly small letters because BIG LETTERS on the internet are rude. Using them is like SHOUTING.

Some people use acronyms in their e-mails. These are a few letters that stand for a longer phrase. They may also use smileys. These are little pictures that tell the other person what you are feeling.

> Time online costs money. Make your messages short. Always ask permission before you send an e-mail.

Say it with a smile

big grin

These are some acronyms that people use. You can make up your own. You can even have secret acronyms that only you and your friends know.

BTW	by the way
CU	see you
DL	download
FYI	for your information
IMO	in my opinion
LOL	laughs out loud
MYOB	mind your own business
OTT	over the top
ROFL	rolls on floor laughing
TIA	thanks in advance
TTFN	ta ta for now
TY	thank you

You make smileys using punctuation marks and keyboard characters. Look at them sideways and you see a face. Here are some smileys. See if you can make up some for yourself.

:-D   big grin   0:-)   angel
:'-(boo hoo   :-P   tongue out
:-(sad   :-{#} smile in a
:-)   happy   brace
;-)   wink   :-O   wow
:-x   not a word $-)   greedy
:-/   what?   :*)   only joking

Smileys are also called emoticons.

Only use an acronym if you know it will be understood. Otherwise you will waste time not save it.

Sending your e-mail

Ben is ready to send his message. He checks the address and subject and clicks on Send. The computer dials up the service provider and the message whizzes off to Hari.

If the computer cannot get online immediately, it saves the message and tries again later. A message on the screen tells you whether your message has been sent or is waiting to go.

If you like, you can send the same message to more than one person at the same time.

To save money, save your messages. Send them all together when you next go online.

Under the address box you will see another box saying 'cc'. In it you write the addresses of all the other people you want the same message to go to. The computer will send the message to all of them at once.

You can also send lots of different messages at one time.

Ben finds the e-mail addresses of some more of his and Liza's friends. He sends them all a message.

Looking for a message

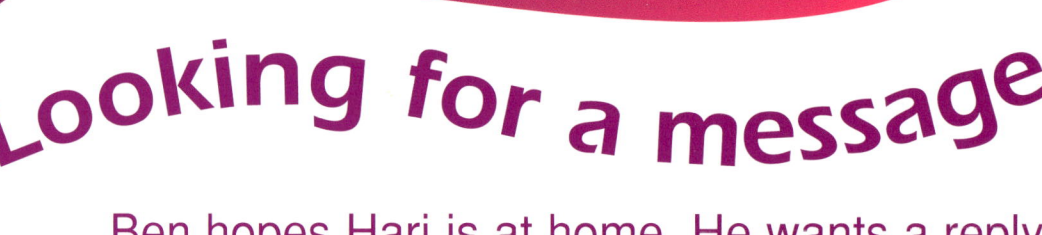

Ben hopes Hari is at home. He wants a reply. Liza shows him how to check the mailbox and tells him the password.

To find out if you have a message, you have to go online and use a password. Ben opens the e-mail window on his computer and clicks on the item that searches for new mail.
He keys in the password.

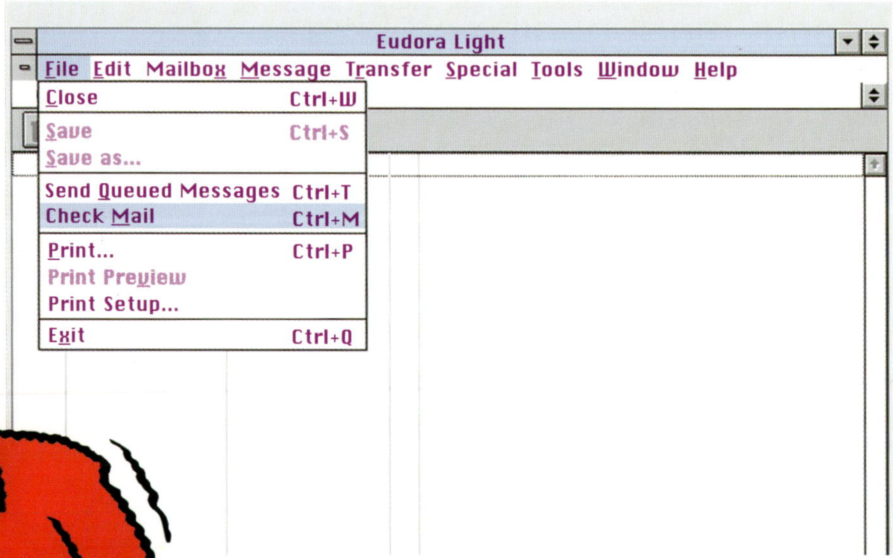

After a while a message comes on the screen. It says that there's no new mail. Ben disconnects from the service provider and waits.

He tries again and again and there is still no reply.

> You can e-mail anyone with an e-mail address – your favourite popstar or even Father Christmas. Don't be disappointed if they are too busy to reply.

Receiving a message

At last! Ben tries once more before bedtime. This time the computer says that there is a message.

Ben watches as the message arrives. It comes in to his mailbox and tells him the sender, subject and date. He clicks on the box and the full message appears on the screen.

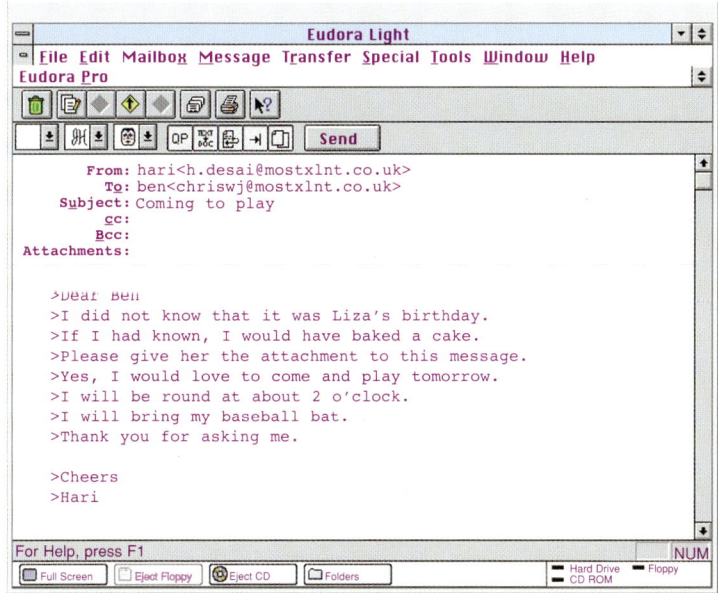

To save money, disconnect from the service provider before you read your messages.

Attachments

Ben is pleased to get Hari's message. He looks for the attachment. It is on his hard disk. It is a file named 'Liza's card'. He double-clicks on the file and up comes a picture on the screen. Ben prints out the file and keeps it for the next day.

You can print out any e-mail message and some attachments.
You do it in the same way that you print any document.

You can send all kinds of things as attachments.

- Any file on your computer.
- A drawing or a birthday card like Hari's.
- Sounds and videos.
- Pictures copied with a scanner.
- Photos taken with a digital camera.

Some e-mail programs let you drag the attachment on to your message. Some use a menu or dialog box to attach the file.

Sending a reply

Next morning Ben checks the mailbox again. There are lots of messages and lots of attachments. They are all birthday messages and cards for Liza.

Liza reads them all and replies to them. It is easy to reply to e-mail messages.

You click on the reply item on the menu. Then you open the mailbox and click on the message you want to reply to.

 # Reply

The message will appear with the address of the sender already in place. You can delete the message if you want to or leave it.

Write your reply in its place or underneath. Then click on Send and off it goes.

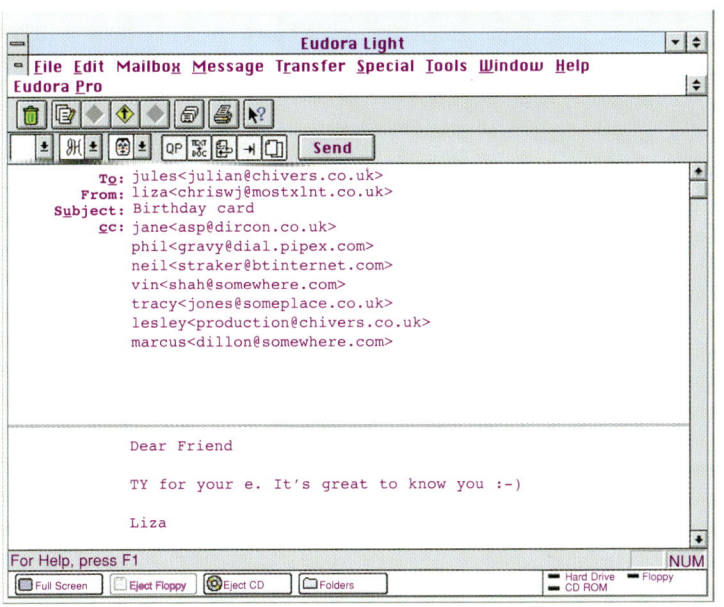

Liza sends one message to all her friends.

Surprise, Surprise!

It is 2 o'clock. Liza's friends come to take her out. But she is not going out. She is having a party.

Ben has sent e-mail invitations to all her friends and all his friends.

"Here they come!" says the Magic Mouse.
"Here they come!" says Mum.

Happy Birthday Liza.

Always ask before you invite anyone to your house.
Never arrange to meet anyone you don't know.

More about e-mail

@ Stands for the word 'at'.

Acronyms Initials used in place of whole words to save time.

Address Everyone on the internet has an address. The first part of an e-mail address is the user name, the second part is the symbol @, the third part is the domain which tells you where the computer is. Only give your e-mail address to people you already know.

Address book Your software program lets you keep a file of names and e-mail addresses. You can type them in or copy them from e-mails you receive. Then when you want to send an e-mail all you need to do is click on the name and the message window will be prepared.

Attachment Any file from your computer that you attach to an e-mail. It can be text or a picture or an animated cartoon or sounds or videos or photographs. Keep attachments small to save time uploading and downloading

Bouncing mail If you get an address wrong or if an address has changed, your message will bounce back to your mailbox.

cc To send a message to more than one person, fill in the other addresses in the cc box on your message heading and everyone you name will receive the e-mail.

Clicking Pressing and quickly releasing the mouse button. To double-click, quickly press and release the button twice. You will soon get to know when you need to click once or twice.

Co Short for 'company'.

Dialog box Window that lets you choose what you want to do next.

Digital camera A camera linked direct to your computer. You can take a picture, plug the camera into the computer and see the picture on-screen immediately or send it as an attachment.

Domain Part of an address that says what type of organisation the computer is in and where it is. The Magic Mouse's computer is in the United Kingdom.

Download When a message or other item is copied from the internet or from another computer to your computer, it downloads.

E-mail Electronic mail.

Emoticons Another name for smileys. It is made up of two words: emotion and icons.

File A single document or computer program.

Folder Place where you keep a group of files.

Flaming If you use CAPITALS or are rude, you may receive angry messages called flame mail.

Header The top part of an e-mail message that tells you about the sender, subject and receiver.

Icon A picture on your computer that you can open by double-clicking.

Internet A worldwide network of millions of linked computers.

Internet service provider A company that you pay to provide a telephone link to the internet.

ISP Short for internet service provider.

Junk mail Advertisements and other unwanted mail that arrives unexpectedly. It is best to throw it away.

Mailbox The place where your computer stores incoming and outgoing e-mail messages.

Mailing lists Lists of people who share an interest and send each other articles. There are hundreds of topics to choose from. If you join a mailing list, you can talk to lots of people. You will also receive lots of mail that you may not want. So be careful before you put your address on a mailing list.

Menu A list of items for you to select from.

Modem An electronic device that sends computer signals through a telephone line.

Netiquette Good manners on the net, including being brief and being polite.

Online When you are linked to the internet, you are online. When you are not linked, you are offline.

Password A set of characters and/or numbers that you key in to the computer to tell the service provider that it is you, not a nosey-parker, who wants to read your messages.

Program Set of electronic instructions that tells your computer what to do.

Punctuation marks Full stops, commas, colons, question marks, quotation marks, like these – . , : ? " – that help make what you write easy to read.

Queue When your service provider cannot get online immediately your message stays in a queue.

Re:Mail See Reply

Reply A quick way to send a reply to an e-mail. The To and Subject boxes are filled in for you. All you have to do is write your message and press Reply or Re:Mail.

Safety There are strange people on the internet. Some adults pretend to be children so be careful.

- Never tell anyone where you live or where you go to school.
- Never give anyone your phone number.
- Never give anyone your password.
- Never arrange to meet anyone you do not already know.
- Never meet anyone without asking your parents first.

Scanner An electronic device that copies text or pictures on to your computer.

Send The icon or menu item you select to send your message.

Service provider Short for internet service provider.

Shouting Using CAPITAL LETTERS instead of small letters.

Signature A special way to sign your e-mails that you can create with some e-mail programs. You can use keyboard characters to draw your face.

Smileys A picture made from keyboard characters that tells the reader what you are feeling. Also called emoticons.

Software Computer programs that you can use for various purposes. You need one to send e-mails.

Sounds You can record or download music and other sounds on to your computer and, if you have the right programs and equipment, attach them to e-mails.

Spamming Sometimes silly people send lots of rude messages to one person. This is called spamming.

Videos If you have the right equipment and programs, you can send videos as attachments to your e-mails.

World wide web Collection of pages, or sites, on the internet that anyone with the right equipment can see.

Index

acronyms 13-15
address 8-11
address box 17
attachments 22, 23, 24

big letters 13
bounce 11

computer 6, 7

digital camera 23
document 23

file 22

icon 10
internet 7, 8
internet service provider 9, 19, 21
ISP 9

mailbox 11, 21, 24
menu 24
message icon 10
modem 6, 7

new mail 18, 19, 20

password 18
photos 23
printing 22, 23
program 6, 10
punctuation marks 15

receiving 20, 21
reply 24

scanner 23
sending 16, 17
short message 12, 13
smileys 13, 15
software program 6
sounds 23

videos 23